AN EASY-READ FACT BOOK

Flags

David Jefferis

Franklin Watts
London   New York   Toronto   Sydney

© 1985 Franklin Watts Ltd

First published in Great Britain
   1985 by
Franklin Watts Ltd
12a Golden Square
London W1

First published in the USA by
Franklin Watts Inc.
387 Park Avenue South
New York
N.Y. 10016

UK ISBN: 0 86313 275 8
US ISBN: 0-531-10008-1
Library of Congress Catalog Card
   Number: 85-50174

Illustrated by
Michael Roffe
Hayward Art Group
Hayward and Martin
Rob Burns
Eagle Artists

Photographs supplied by
All Sport
Mary Evans Picture Library
Daily Telegraph Colour Library

Technical consultant
William Crampton,
The Flag Institute

Printed in Great Britain by
Cambus Litho, East Kilbride

Flags

Contents

The first flags

△This Roman soldier of 2,000 years ago is carrying a vexillum. This type of flag was used mainly by troops of cavalry so they could identify each other at a distance.

The origin of the earliest flags is lost [in the mists of time,] but we know they have been used for 5,000 years or more.

In 3,000 BC, the ancient Chinese made flags of silk for military and religious occasions. The Romans used flags as identifying badges for their horse-mounted cavalry soldiers.

In the Middle Ages, the largest battle flags were hauled to war on heavy wheeled carts. They had a guard of the best soldiers to protect them.

Such was the importance of an army's flag of "color," that if it fell or was captured, the result was usually retreat or surrender. If a battle was going badly, the flag became a rallying point around which troops could gather their strength.

Today's flags are not quite so vital to us, but they can still unite people who believe in the idea or country the flag represents.

The raven symbol was possibly carried on Viking raiders' flags in the 9th century.

The Knights of St. John used this Maltese Cross in the Middle Ages.

Columbus used this flag on his voyage to America in 1492.

△The battle scene above, at Crecy, France in 1327, shows the way flags were used on battlefields in the Middle Ages. Below you see other flags of the past.

5

Flags of the world

On this, and the following pages, are the flags of the world's nations. The flag of Denmark is thought to be the oldest, dating back to about 1219. Those of many newly independent African, Caribbean or Pacific countries are very recent. Vanuatu, for example, became independent in 1980.

Afghanistan

Albania

Algeria

Andorra

Angola

Antigua and Barbuda

Anguilla (unofficial)

Argentina

Australia

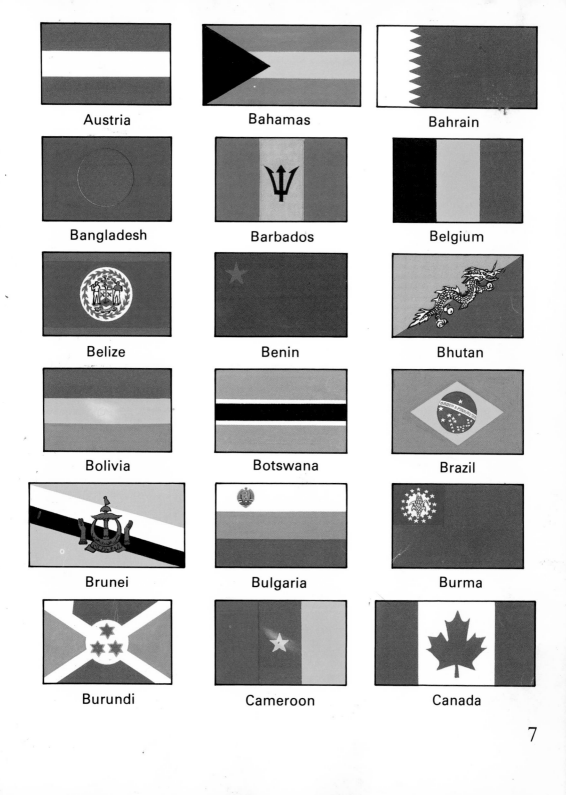

Austria

Bahamas

Bahrain

Bangladesh

Barbados

Belgium

Belize

Benin

Bhutan

Bolivia

Botswana

Brazil

Brunei

Bulgaria

Burma

Burundi

Cameroon

Canada

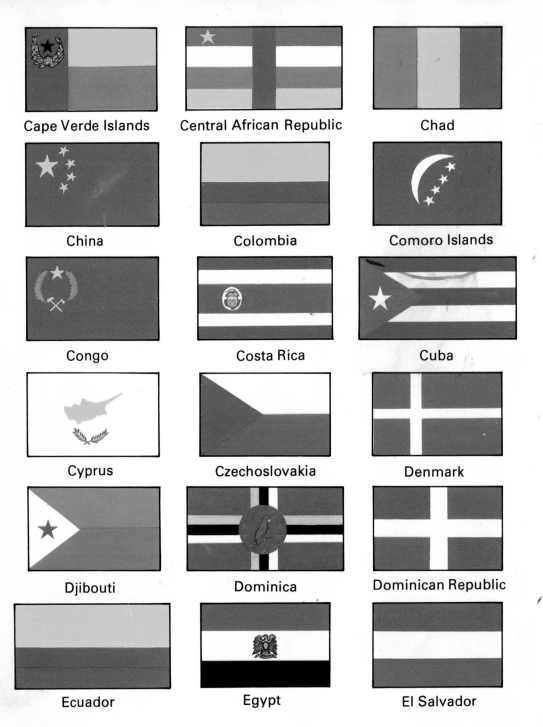

Cape Verde Islands	Central African Republic	Chad
China	Colombia	Comoro Islands
Congo	Costa Rica	Cuba
Cyprus	Czechoslovakia	Denmark
Djibouti	Dominica	Dominican Republic
Ecuador	Egypt	El Salvador

Equatorial Guinea	Ethiopia	Fiji
Finland	France	Gabon
Germany (East)	Germany (West)	Ghana
Greece	Grenada	Guatemala
Guinea	Guinea-bissau	Guyana
Haiti	Honduras	Hungary

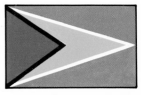

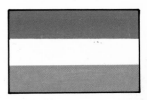
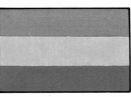
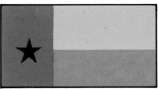

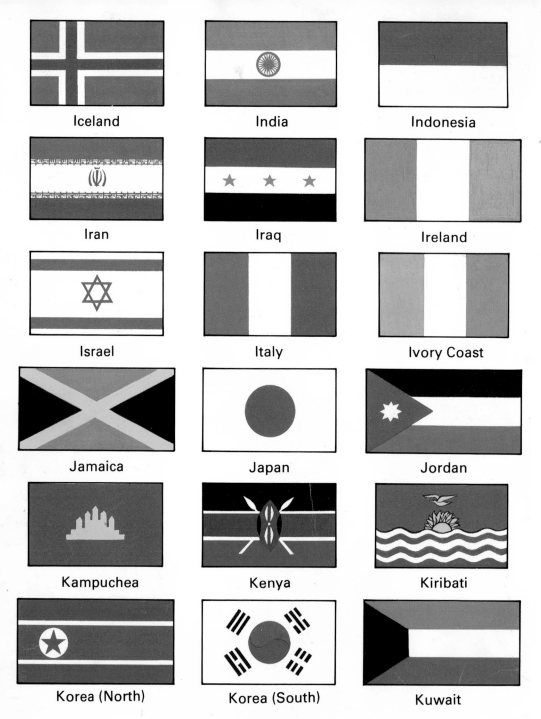

Iceland	India	Indonesia
Iran	Iraq	Ireland
Israel	Italy	Ivory Coast
Jamaica	Japan	Jordan
Kampuchea	Kenya	Kiribati
Korea (North)	Korea (South)	Kuwait

10

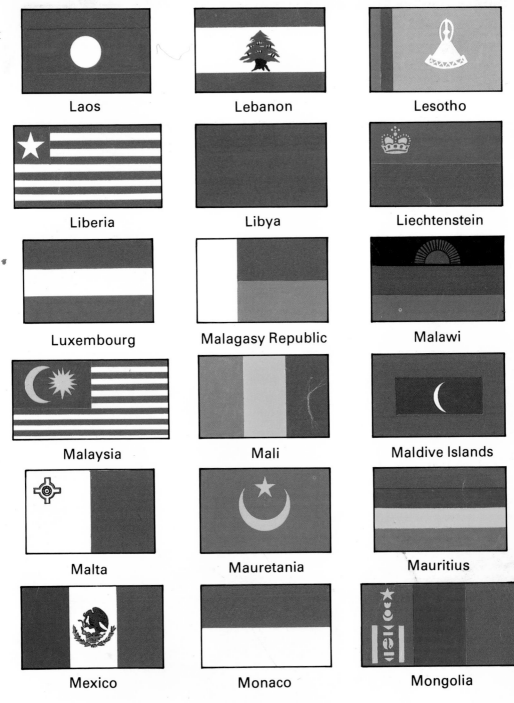

Laos	Lebanon	Lesotho
Liberia	Libya	Liechtenstein
Luxembourg	Malagasy Republic	Malawi
Malaysia	Mali	Maldive Islands
Malta	Mauretania	Mauritius
Mexico	Monaco	Mongolia

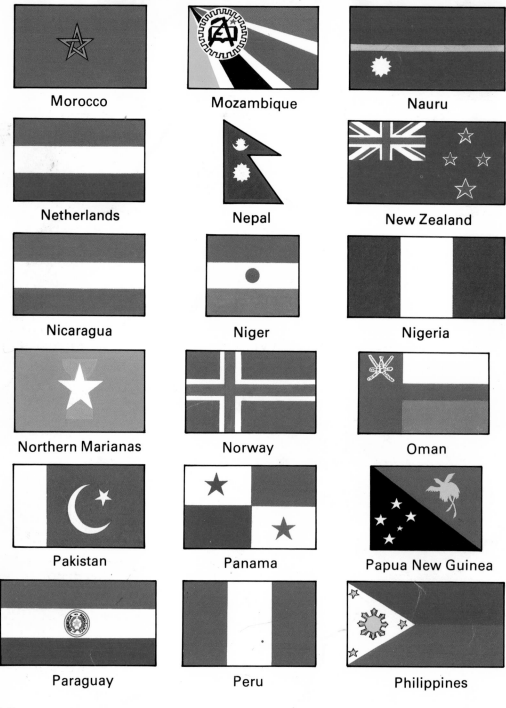

Morocco

Mozambique

Nauru

Netherlands

Nepal

New Zealand

Nicaragua

Niger

Nigeria

Northern Marianas

Norway

Oman

Pakistan

Panama

Papua New Guinea

Paraguay

Peru

Philippines

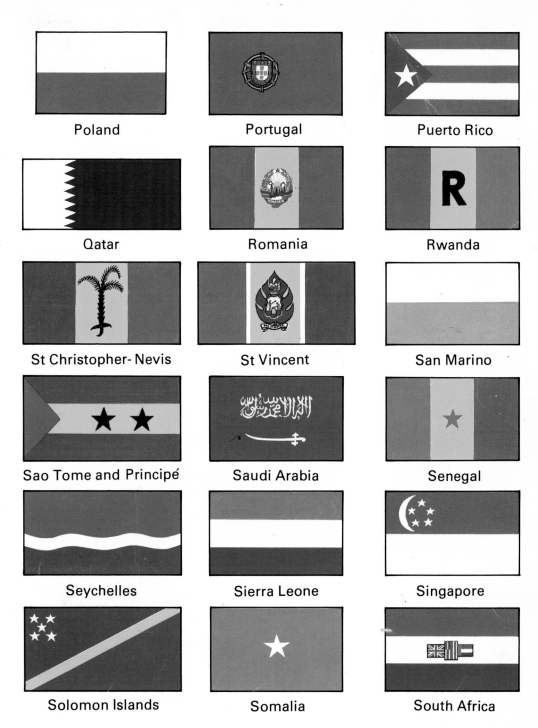

Poland

Portugal

Puerto Rico

Qatar

Romania

Rwanda

St Christopher-Nevis

St Vincent

San Marino

Sao Tome and Principé

Saudi Arabia

Senegal

Seychelles

Sierra Leone

Singapore

Solomon Islands

Somalia

South Africa

13

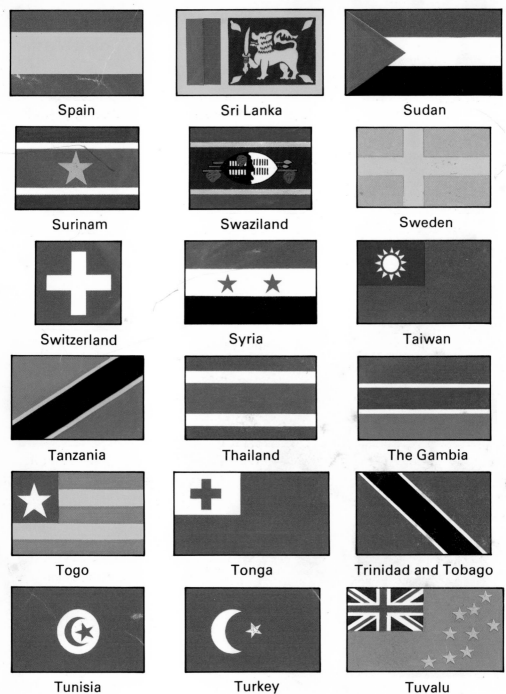

Spain

Sri Lanka

Sudan

Surinam

Swaziland

Sweden

Switzerland

Syria

Taiwan

Tanzania

Thailand

The Gambia

Togo

Tonga

Trinidad and Tobago

Tunisia

Turkey

Tuvalu

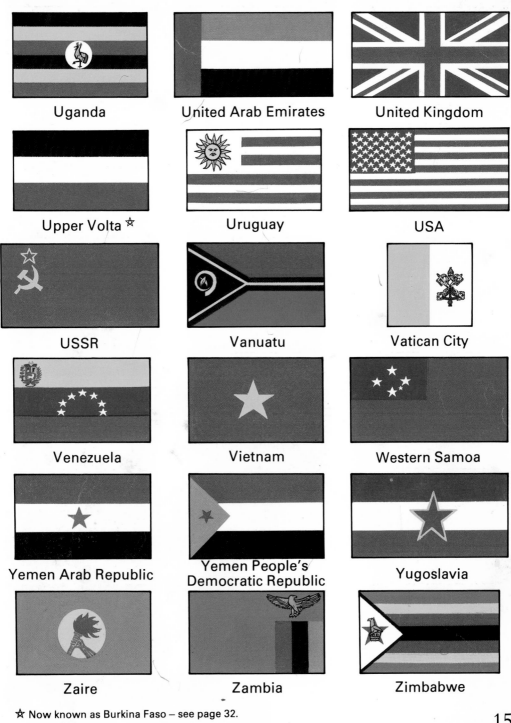

Uganda

United Arab Emirates

United Kingdom

Upper Volta ☆

Uruguay

USA

USSR

Vanuatu

Vatican City

Venezuela

Vietnam

Western Samoa

Yemen Arab Republic

Yemen People's
Democratic Republic

Yugoslavia

Zaire

Zambia

Zimbabwe

☆ Now known as Burkina Faso – see page 32.

Flag shapes

▽ The Inglefield clip can be used to attach a flag to ropes, used to haul it up and down the flagstaff.

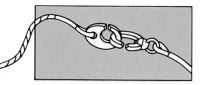

All national flags, except that of Nepal, are plain rectangles. But many shapes and sizes are possible. You can see a typical variety of them on these pages.

A pennant is a small triangular flag. Flags can also have swallowtails, named after the twin-tail of the bird.

The parts of a flag

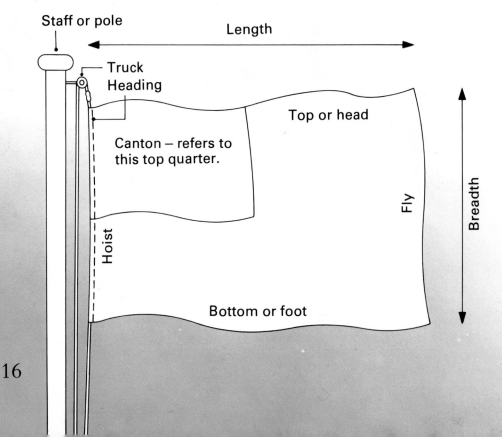

Staff or pole

Length

Truck
Heading

Top or head

Canton – refers to this top quarter.

Fly

Breadth

Hoist

Bottom or foot

16

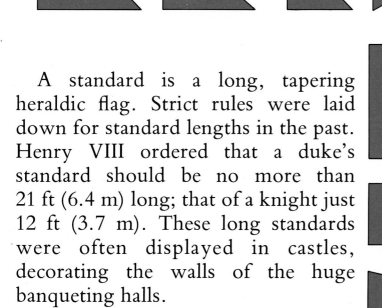

Pennant

Swallowtail

A standard is a long, tapering heraldic flag. Strict rules were laid down for standard lengths in the past. Henry VIII ordered that a duke's standard should be no more than 21 ft (6.4 m) long; that of a knight just 12 ft (3.7 m). These long standards were often displayed in castles, decorating the walls of the huge banqueting halls.

A banner is usually the personal flag of a person or group. But "standard" is also commonly used to mean a personal banner.

Signals at sea

△The "Jolly Roger," with its skull and crossbones, was used as a bloodthirsty symbol by pirates. An early flag used a devil holding a spear. Nowadays submarine crews have used it to show they have sunk a ship. The white flag is a universal symbol of truce.

Signal flags were first used systematically in the 1700s. They are still in use, though the patterns and meanings are much changed. The alphabet of flags on the right is the present-day International Flag Code. Some flags have other meanings if flown on their own. The P or "Blue Peter" is flown to show that a ship is about to sail. The yellow Q is flown to show that there is disease on board and the ship is in quarantine.

Ships' flags are flown from various places. The jack (at the bow) and ensign (at the stern) are national flags. Merchant ships fly a house flag, which often contains the same company badge or logo painted on the funnel.

Warships fly masthead pennants and, when in port, the personal flags of the high-ranking officers aboard. In a sea battle, if one side lowers its national flag completely, this is a sign of surrender.

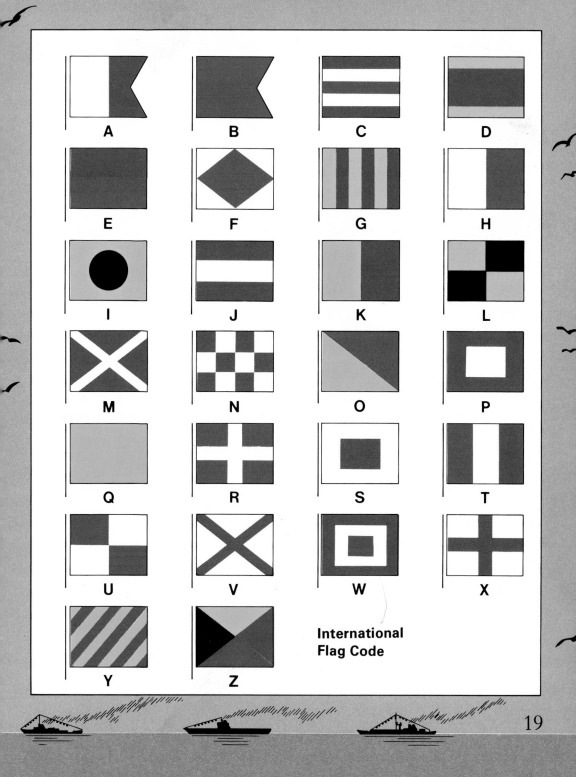

International
Flag Code

International flags

United Nations

Organization of African Unity

Olympic Games

Organization of American States

△Shown here are just a few important international flags.

Many flags are designed to represent organizations which have links between different countries.

Probably the best known is the Olympic flag. The joined circles represent people of the five continents. The flag has been used since 1906.

The United Nations flag uses a world globe, circled by a pair of olive branches. These symbolize peace, one

20

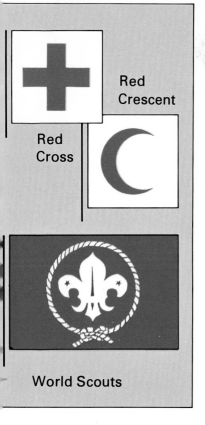

Red Cross

Red Crescent

World Scouts

of the aims of the UN.

A red cross on a white background is used by ambulances, hospitals and medical teams in war. It was first used in 1863 and various other countries have similar flags. In muslim lands, the Red Crescent is used. Israel uses a red six-sided Star of David. Russia adds a red crescent alongside the cross.

△Flags are used as the basis for many commercial designs. The Greek Olympic Airways adds one circle to the five "Games" circles which are painted on the tails of all its planes.

Flags of heads of state

△In Great Britain, flags are displayed at many state occasions. Here, Brazilian flags are flown alongside those of Great Britain as a mark of respect to Brazil's visiting premier.

These flags are flown as the personal standard of the person chosen to lead a country. These people always used to be kings and queens. Today few royal families have any say in the day-to-day running of a country. But they conduct many ceremonies and appear at state occasions where flags may be an important part of the event. On the right you can see a variety of personal flags, belonging to European royal families, Presidents and an Emperor.

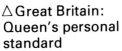

△ Great Britain:
Queen's personal
standard

△ Netherlands:
Royal standard

△ Japan: Emperor

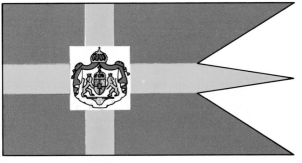

△ Sweden: Royal
standard

△ United States of America:
President

△ West Germany:
President

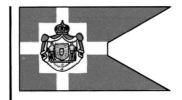

△ Denmark: Queen's
Royal standard

△ Egypt: President

Changing flags

▽ This chart shows how the Union flag of Britain developed. Strictly speaking, it should only be called the Union Jack when it is flown at the bows of a ship. Opposite, you can see how the Stars and Stripes developed.

Many national flags have changed over the years, as countries have grown or changed in some way.

In 1603, England and Scotland joined in a union. The new flag, chosen in 1606, was the red cross of England, combined with the St. Andrew's cross of Scotland. In 1801, the cross of St.

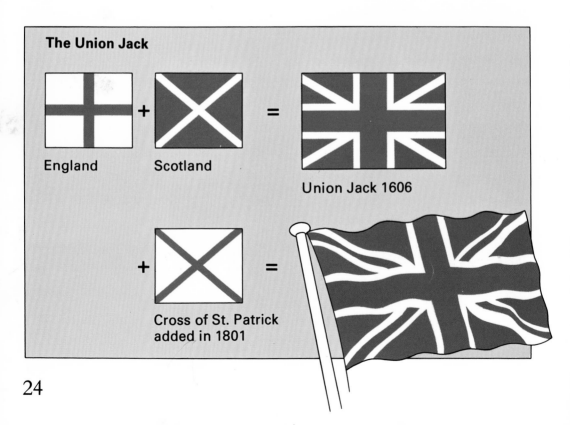

The Union Jack

England + Scotland = Union Jack 1606

+ Cross of St. Patrick added in 1801 =

Patrick was added, to form the familiar Union Flag of today.

The American flag developed in the War of Independence. Earlier flags were used by various rebel groups, but the "Stars and Stripes" was first flown in 1777. It had 13 stars, representing the colonies which broke away from Britain. There are now 50 stars. Each one represents a state of the union.

The French Tricolor became a symbol of freedom, as it was adopted after the French Revolution of 1789.

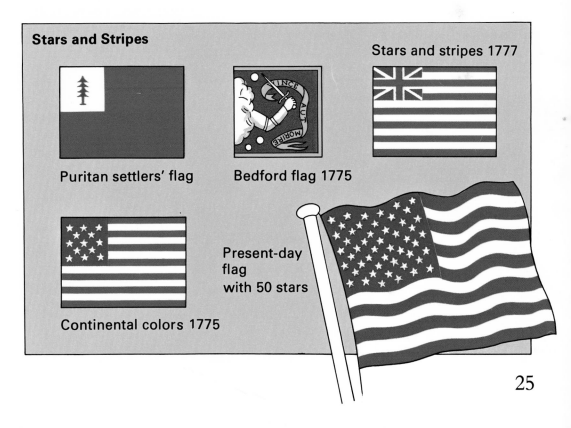

Stars and Stripes

Stars and stripes 1777

Puritan settlers' flag

Bedford flag 1775

Continental colors 1775

Present-day flag with 50 stars

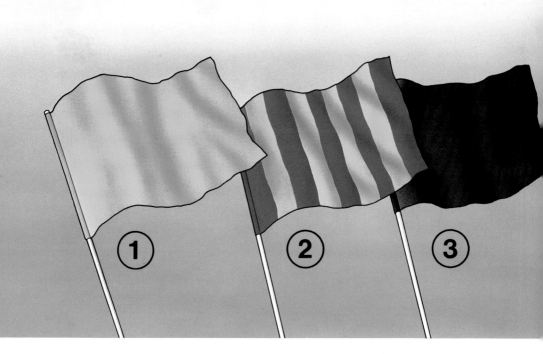

Motor racing flags

△Here are some race track flags.
1 Caution, danger ahead.
2 Oil on the track.
3 Must call in at pit.
4 Race must stop.
5 Let a faster driver overtake.
6 Ambulance or other official vehicle on track.
7 Finish.

Motor racing flags are used by track marshals and other race officials to signal clearly to the drivers.

The start of a race used to be signalled by the downward wave of a flag, generally the national flag of the country where the race was held. Today, starting–signal light systems are mostly

used on all but small tracks.

Trouble on the track is shown by a variety of flags. Yellow indicates danger ahead – perhaps an obstruction on the track. Red and yellow stripes indicate oil on the circuit. A black flag is an order to pull in at the pits, the service bays near the starting line. There are other flags too, and you can see them in the picture below.

The finish is always shown by the wave of a black-and-white checkered flag as the winner crosses the line.

△A track marshal waits with his checkered flag at the ready.

27

Flag design

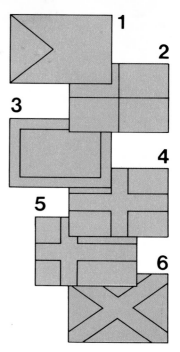

Some of today's flags originated with the heraldry or coats of arms of powerful families of the Middle Ages.

Knights began to put "arms," signs and pictures, on their shields. They were needed in battle, as a knight was unrecognizable in his helmet and armor. The knights could not have the same arms, so strict rules of heraldry were laid down. These decided what the arms meant and who could wear them. The system came from Normandy, in France, so all the terms have roots in the French language.

Many heraldic designs were imprinted on banners carried by medieval knights into battle. Early European flags were strongly influenced by heraldic designs and even today certain heraldic ideas and styles can be found in the flags of the world.

△Flag patterns include the ones shown here.
1 Triangle
2 Quarterly
3 Border
4 Cross
5 Scandinavian cross
6 Saltire

▷On the page opposite, you can see how heraldic shields were divided and some examples of charges.

Divisions of heraldic shields

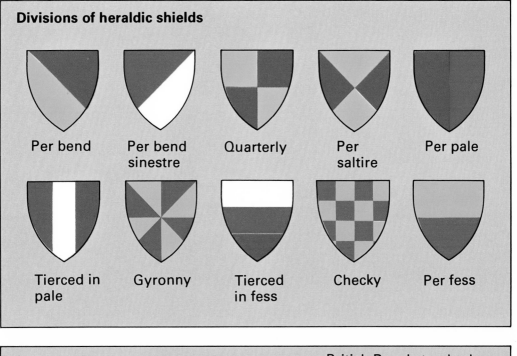

Per bend	Per bend sinestre	Quarterly

Per saltire

Per pale

Tierced in pale

Gyronny

Tierced in fess

Checky

Per fess

Symbols and charges

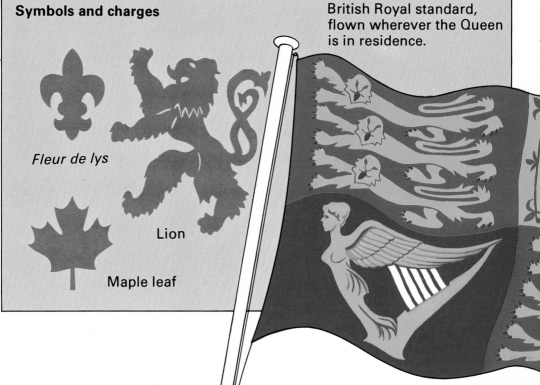

British Royal standard, flown wherever the Queen is in residence.

Fleur de lys

Lion

Maple leaf

Flag words

Here is a list of some of the technical words used in this book.

Arms
The name given to the signs and symbols of heraldry. Arms were first put on the shields of knights to show who they were.

Banner
The personal flag of a person or group.

Blue Peter
Name for the P flag of the International Flag Code. Flown when a ship is about to set sail. Other naval flags include the yellow Q – traditionally flown to show "plague aboard." It has a similar meaning now; it shows the ship is in quarantine – "infectious disease aboard."

Charge
Pictures and symbols of heraldry. Examples include the lion of England, the maple leaf of Canada and a Masai warrior shield, found on the flag of Kenya.

Color
The word used for the flag of a particular military unit such as an army regiment.

Flagstaff
Official name for the flagpole.

Fly
Part of a flag furthest from the flagstaff.

Halyards
The ropes used to haul a flag up and down the flagstaff. A flag flown at half-mast is a sign of mourning for someone who has just died.

Heraldry
The rules laid down in the Middle Ages governing the coats of arms used by knights. To avoid confusion no two knights could use the same arms when they had their armor and helmets on.

Today there are clubs and societies devoted to re-enacting the battles and tournaments of the Middle Ages. If you get to see a public display you can see the brightly colored arms of old in the 20th century.

Hoist
Part of a flag nearest the flagstaff.

Jack
Flag flown at the front, or bow, of a ship. The ship's ensign is flown from the stern.

Jolly Roger
Nickname given to the skull and crossbones flag flown by pirates.

Pennant
Small triangular flag.

The semaphore system

Standard
The banner of a head of state or royalty.

Stars and Stripes
The US national flag. From having just 13 stars when it was first introduced, the flag now boasts a total of 50, each representing a state of the union.

Vexillology
Word used to describe the study of flags. A flag expert is called a vexillologist.

Vexillum
Flag used by the Roman army, carried on the end of a lance. The exact date of its introduction is unknown, but likely to have been about 100 B.C.

The vexillum was usually purple or red, but sometimes came in blue or white. It was the only "flag" in the modern sense until the Raven flag of the Vikings was devised. This was first recorded in the year 878 A.D.

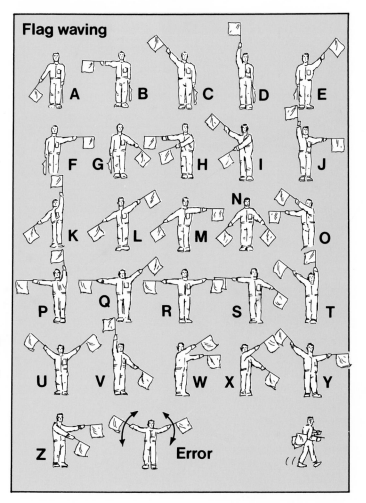

Flag waving

△Here you see the semaphore flag alphabet. It was invented before the days of radio. Navies used semaphore for communicating between ships and for ship-to-shore messages.

Index

Burkina Faso is the new name for Upper Volta. The flag has a gold star on a red (top) and dark green (bottom) background.

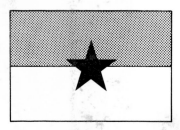